# THE ROOTS OF THE
# REFORMATION

CANTERBURY BOOKS

# THE ROOTS OF THE REFORMATION

by
KARL ADAM

Translated by
CECILY HASTINGS

SHEED & WARD · NEW YORK

SHEED AND WARD INC.
840 BROADWAY
NEW YORK 3

NIHIL OBSTAT: MICHAEL P. NOONAN, S.M.
CENSOR DEPUTATUS
IMPRIMATUR: ✠ RICHARD J. CUSHING
ARCHBISHOP OF BOSTON
BOSTON, MARCH 22, 1951

This book is a large part of *One and Holy,* a
translation of *Una Sancta in katholischer Sicht,*
published by Patmos-Verlag, Düsseldorf.

Manufactured in the United States of America

# CONTENTS

# I

## WEAKNESS IN THE CHURCH

*Rome*

ODERN historians are agreed that the roots of the Reformation reach far back into the high Middle Ages. The former monk of Cluny, Gregory VII, in his zeal for the liberty and reform of the Church, so interpreted the papal claims formulated by Augustine, Gregory the Great and Nicholas I that right up into the late Middle Ages they excited repeated resistance from the secular powers, shook the prestige of the Papal See and so prepared the way for Luther's Reformation. Gregory's *Dictatus Papae*, in which he claimed for the Pope a direct authority even over secular affairs, with the right to depose unworthy princes and release their subjects from their oath of allegiance, inspired papal policy all through the Middle Ages.

This certainly added a corrosive bitterness and a devastating violence—a violence which did not stop short of the Papal See itself—to the conflicts which in any event would have been bitter enough between

*Regnum* and *Sacerdotium*, the struggle between the Emperor Henry IV and the Pope over investitures, the battles with the Hohenstaufen, Frederick Barbarossa and Frederick II, the conflicts with Philip the Fair of France and Ludwig of Bavaria. In Frederick II's Manifesto of 1230 Gregory IX is already branded as "the great Dragon and Antichrist of the last days". In 1301 Philip the Fair had Boniface VIII's Bull *Ausculta* publicly burned, and in 1303 had the Pope himself taken into custody as a "heretic, blasphemer and simoniac". Ludwig of Bavaria, supported by the Franciscan Spirituals, declared Pope John XXII a "formal heretic" in the Reichstag at Nuremberg in 1323.

The counter-attack of the "spiritual sword" was a series of excommunications, extending to the fourth degree of kindred, and years of interdict over whole countries. Germany alone was under interdict for twenty years, which meant that no public religious service could be held, no sacrament could be publicly administered, no bell could sound. The more often these ecclesiastical penalties were imposed, the blunter grew the spiritual sword. Inevitably the religion and morality of the people suffered serious damage, their sense of the Church was weakened, their sympathies were alienated from Christ's vicar. In due course there arose theologians amongst the Franciscan Spirituals, particularly their

General Michael of Cesena, and William of Ockham, who in numerous writings questioned the founding by Christ of the Papacy as the Church knows it. And Marsilius of Padua in 1324 drew up a revolutionary programme entitled *Defensor Pacis*, with a theory of Church and State which broke completely with existing ecclesiastical constitutions —"a significant prelude to the Reformation".[1]

Anti-papal feeling in Germany gained ground when, in 1314, the See of Rome moved to Avignon and was thus brought completely under French influence, and again when the financial burdens arising out of the double establishment at Rome and Avignon compelled the Pope to build up a system of taxation which, when expanded, weighed heavily both on spiritual and on economic life. The Camera Apostolica covered the whole Church with a net of taxation called the Census. Besides the revenues of the Papal State, this included pallium-money (the

[1] Since Luther can only be understood against the background of the ecclesiastical abuses of the late Middle Ages, I could not avoid dealing with these abuses in detail. I have deliberately taken my evidence exclusively from Catholic sources, especially from Karl Bihlmeyer's history of the Church (the objectivity and thoroughness of which have made it the standard work on the subject), and Josef Lortz's brilliant and psychologically penetrating *Reformation in Deutschland*. In the light of recent researches it should hardly be necessary to emphasize that these abuses do not give the whole picture of the medieval Church. Its darker aspects are relieved by so many bright lights that it is not possible to take a pessimistic view of it as a whole.

The quotation is from the second volume of Bihlmeyer's work, p. 356.

tax paid by newly appointed archbishops, bishops and abbots), *spolia* (the total assets of deceased prelates), the numerous administrative taxes and procurations for papal visitations; above all, the taxes on the revenues of vacant benefices, and annates (payment of the first year's income, or at least half of it, from all ecclesiastical appointments made by the Pope). Since Clement IV had claimed for the Pope unlimited authority over all ecclesiastical appointments in Christendom, the number of benefices reserved to the Pope had risen beyond computation. This aroused general opposition, especially when John XXII, in the course of his conflict with Ludwig of Bavaria, tried to fill all the vacant sees and offices in Germany with his own supporters.

In a similar spirit, but contrary to prevailing ecclesiastical law, the Papal Chancellery in the fourteenth and fifteenth centuries encouraged *cumulus beneficiorum*, i.e., the holding of many benefices by one person, and commendation, by which a benefice could be conferred simply for the income derived from it, without the holder's having any spiritual obligations to fulfil. Moreover, the Pope could promise to provide a person to a benefice even before its present occupant had actually died. The spirit of mammon had won such an ascendancy in the Curia that Pope Clement VII, for example, at the very height of the Reformation storm, was trying to make money from the sale of Cardinals' hats. It is against this background that we must understand the denunciation of the great Catholic preacher Geiler von Kaisersberg: "It is no longer the Holy Ghost who appoints the rulers of the Church, but the devil, and for money, for favour and by bribery of the Cardinals."[1]

It is easily understandable that the Curia's irresponsible policies in matters of taxation and appointments, together with the arbitrary occupation of ecclesiastical offices in Germany by foreigners, gravely limited orderly diocesan government, and that they aroused on all sides uncertainty in regard to the law and consequent discontent amounting to unrest and resistance. There were expensive lawsuits that had to be taken to the highest papal court, the Roman Rota. The German nation had its public grievances (*gravamina nationis Germanicae*). They were raised for the first time in 1456 by Archbishop Dietrich of Mainz at the Fürstentag at Frankfurt. From then on they came up again and again in the Reichstag in the form in which the humanist Jakob Wimpfeling had consolidated them. But the abuses, so far from being removed, mounted from year to year as the papal requirements increased. The Pope's

---

[1] A less severe judgment on this matter is given by Barraclough, *Papal Provisions*. (Trans.)

11

yearly income was greater than that of any German Emperor. John XXII, for instance, died leaving three-quarters of a million gold coins in his treasury: a figure so high, considering the values and conditions of the time, that it was bound to have a catastrophic effect on the believer when he pictured against this background the poor tent-maker Paul, or the still poorer fisherman Peter, coming with dusty sandals to Rome and bringing nothing with them but a deep and noble desire to preach Christ and to die for Christ.

If the fiscal policy of Avignon, where the Popes had their court for sixty-five years, seriously damaged the political and economic interests of German Christianity and so at least indirectly undermined the religious authority of the Pope, the great Schism of the West, from 1378 to 1417, threatened the prestige of the Papacy with final extinction.

In opposition to Urban VI, elected under pressure from the Roman people and disliked for various reasons, the French Cardinals in Avignon, the so-called "ultramontani", declaring the election unfree and invalid, raised a cousin of the French King to the papal chair as Clement VII, and Christendom was split into two camps. The division went right through the Christian body. Whole Orders, such as the Cistercians, Carthusians, Franciscans, Dominicans and Carmelites, fell into two halves. And since

12

both Popes excommunicated each other and each other's supporters, the whole of Christendom was at least nominally excommunicate. The split did not come to an end with the deaths of the two Popes, for the Cardinals in Rome and Avignon all obstinately held their own papal elections. Matters grew worse when the Council of Pisa, in 1409, deposed both the Rome and the Avignon Popes as "notorious schismatics and heretics" and elected a third, Alexander V, who soon died, and was followed by John XXIII. Since both the deposed Popes obstinately maintained the validity of their elections this led, not to unity, but "from wicked duality to accursed triplicity". It was only in 1417, with the election of Martin V at the Council of Constance, that the Church could acknowledge one single head again in place of the three previously elected claimants.

It was inevitable that this schism of nearly forty years should shake the Church to her foundation; that radicals of the type of William of Ockham and Marsilius of Padua should formulate a democratic theory of the Church, taking the plenitude of ecclesiastical authority to rest in the body of the faithful, not in a single head; that thoughtful theologians such as Peter d'Ailly and the distinguished John Gerson should construct the so-called conciliar theory, making the Pope subordinate to a General Council and giving the Church a parliamentary instead of a monarchical constitution. The idea of the Church received from the Fathers—in which there was but *one* Rock, *one* Keeper of the Keys, *one* Shepherd—began to weaken. Trust in the Father of Christendom was gone. In this sense, the experience of the Great Schism had impressed its decisive stamp on the minds of the faithful (Lortz).

Hard upon the dogmatic attack on papal authority inevitably conjured up by the Great Western Schism, there followed its moral collapse; the Renaissance Popes seem to have carried out in their own lives that cult of idolatrous humanism, demonic ambition and unrestrained sensuality which was in many ways bound up with the reawakening of the ancient ideal of manhood. The most sober ecclesiastical historians agree that the reigns of the Popes from Sixtus IV to Leo X "represent, from the religious and ecclesiastical point of view, the lowest level of the Papacy since the tenth and eleventh centuries" (Bihlmeyer, vol. ii, p. 477). The unbridled nepotism of Sixtus IV, which threatened to degrade the Papacy to "a dynastic heritage and the *Patrimonium Petri* to a petty Italian state" (Lortz, vol. i, p. 75), was followed by the fateful Bull against witches issued by Innocent VIII, a man of scandalous life. Worse still was the conduct of Alexander VI, stained with murder and impurity, and the demonic lust

14

for blood and power of his son Cesare Borgia. Then came the burning of the Dominican Savonarola at Alexander's orders, the sheer political jugglery of Julius II, whose pontificate was dissipated in campaigns and wars, and finally the pleasure-loving worldliness of Leo X, who found the chase and the theatre more important than Martin Luther and his religious aspirations. The reputation of the Papacy was dragged not merely in the dust but in the mud. It is especially significant of the mentality of Leo X and of the Renaissance Popes in general, that in the solemn procession at his enthronement in the papal chair, the Most Blessed Sacrament was accompanied by statues of naked pagan gods, with the inscription "First Venus reigned [the age of Alexander VI], then Mars [in the time of Julius II], and now [under Leo X] Pallas Athene holds the sceptre" (Lortz, vol. i, p. 86).

The news of these scandalous doings, of course, soon crossed the Alps and stripped the last vestige of credit from the Mother of Christendom. The humanist circles at Erfurt and Florence took care of that, and so later did Ulrich von Hutten and the Dunkelmänner letters. Nor was Luther himself far behind them. Even when he was translating the Bible in 1522, before he had reached the hey-day of his hatred for Rome, he depicted the great Harlot of the Apocalypse as wearing the triple papal crown.

15

## *Germany*

Let us turn now from the crying scandals surrounding the highest ecclesiastical authority to the abuses which marred the German Church and her spiritual life before Luther's advent.

It is certainly not true to say that the German Church which witnessed these scandals in the Roman government was herself ripe for destruction. The constant urge for reform and the tremendous response when Luther raised the alarm would be incomprehensible if Christian life had died out completely. We can even assert that German Christianity in the last phase of the Middle Ages was, in spite of all, more devout than it is to-day. For to-day a denunciation of abuses by a Martin Luther would cause no revolution. It was the age of the three Catherines, of Siena, Bologna and Genoa; the age when St. Bridget scourged the abuses of the Avignon Curia with the flames of her wrath, when Thomas à Kempis wrote his immortal *Imitation of Christ*, when an unknown priest wrote the *Theologia Germanica* first published by Luther. It was the age in which German mysticism flowered in Eckhardt, Tauler and Suso, and the *devotio moderna* of the "Brothers of the Common Life" was aspiring to revivify, spiritualize and personalize benumbed Christianity.

The evidence grows greater and greater that even the common people of the Church, so long as they had not fallen a prey to sectarianism or been touched by radical humanism, were genuinely devoted to their Catholic faith despite all the abuses, and that daily life remained embedded in religious usage right up to the end of the Middle Ages. Even the simple people then knew how to distinguish between the office and the person's own piety and to apply our Lord's words to the gloomy contemporary scene: "All things therefore whatsoever they shall say to you, observe and do; but according to their works do ye not" (Matt. xxiii. 3).

During this same second half of the fifteenth century, there was an abundance of pious works *ad remedium animae* (for the welfare of souls): new churches were built, new parishes opened, new appointments of preachers made and charitable institutions set up. New religious and charitable brotherhoods were formed, and even new devotions introduced, such as the *Angelus* and the Way of the Cross. There was more catechetical and devotional literature than ever. Booklets and examinations of conscience for Confession, catechism tables, Bible story-books, rhymed Bibles, poor men's Bibles, appeared in the service of religious instruction. Before 1518 a translation of the Bible into High German had run into fourteen editions and one in Low

17

German into four editions. All in all one can fairly speak of an increase of piety in this period. Yet it was seriously lacking in the inner spirit, in the living penetration of pious practices with the spirit of the Gospel. There was too much externalism, too much mere automatism and superficiality, and also far too much unhealthy emotionalism in this piety.

The shepherds and teachers who might have directed and deepened the stream of faith were lacking. The higher clergy were mostly noblemen who had entered the priesthood from material rather than spiritual motives. Bishoprics, prelacies and abbacies had for long been the preserve of the nobility. At the outbreak of the Reformation eighteen bishoprics and archbishoprics in Germany were occupied by the sons of princes. Proof of proficiency in the tourney was an absolutely requisite qualification for most canonries. It is evident that prelates so immersed in worldliness and pleasure had neither the ability nor the desire to break the Bread of Life to the people.

Over against these prelates, "God's Junkers", we see the lower clergy. They seldom had benefices of their own and were compelled either to carry out the duties of a benefice for a pittance from some member of the higher clergy, or earn their living by helping to serve Mass and doing odd jobs about the church. Their economic position was therefore extremely precarious. Their theological training was no better. Excepting the handful of the clergy who were educated at the universities, most of them contented themselves with a modest smattering of religion, Latin and liturgy. Their morals were not much better than their theological knowledge. One could hardly expect a higher moral standard from them than the example set by their superiors. Documentary evidence indicates that there was amongst them much brutality, drunkenness, gambling, avarice, simony and superstition. To secure a living for themselves they exacted almost insupportable fees for the slightest exercise of their priesthood, even from the poor and destitute. The charge for the administration of the Last Sacraments was so high that Extreme Unction was called "the Sacrament of the rich". Concubinage was so general that at the Councils of Constance and Basel the Emperor Sigismund proposed the abolition of the law of celibacy.

Amidst the general decline there were still of course plenty of morally upright priests. The humanist Jakob Wimpfeling, a severely critical observer of the life of the Church, vouched "before God" to knowing in the six dioceses of the Rhine "many, nay innumerable, chaste and learned prelates and clergy, of unblemished reputation, full of piety, liberality and care for the poor" (Lortz, vol.

i, p. 90). We need only call to mind the illustrious figure of the saintly Nicholas of Cusa, the herald of the modern age and tireless reformer, who sought over and over again by visitations, by word of mouth, and in his writings, to communicate his own spirit of piety to the German Church. But to most of the clergy we must apply the words of Pope Adrian VI in his first consistorial address, quoting from St. Bernard: "Vice has grown so much a matter of course that those who are stained with it are no longer aware of the stink of sin."

The regular clergy were no better than the seculars. Here too we must, of course, beware of false generalizations. It was precisely in this second half of the fifteenth century that almost all the older Orders made an effort to reform. In the case of the Benedictines there were, for example, the reforms of Kastl, Melk and Bursfeld. All the Mendicant Orders still had houses in which the original lofty spirit of the love of God and neighbour was alive. And again and again a saint would arise somewhere in the Church, like Bernardino of Siena, John Capistran the lover of souls, and the noble Caritas Pirkheimer, who were shining examples of Christian piety. Luther's account of his own experiences in the Augustinian Priory at Erfurt gives the lie to the statement that monastic discipline was in a universal decline. It is also significant that later on it was ex-

monks in particular who were among Luther's best
co-operators—who were among the most impatient,
in fact, of current abuses.

Nevertheless, we have from within the Church
enough official and unofficial testimony to give us a
gloomy picture of life in the Orders. Amongst the
more ancient Orders only the Carthusians and in
part the Cistercians really maintained their original
standard. In the other monasteries there was a tragic
decline in discipline. The great Benedictine abbeys
had become a mere convenience of the nobility. But
in the Mendicant Orders, too, the foundations of
the religious life had begun to totter—not least on
account of the irresponsible caprice with which the
officials of the Curia at Avignon dispensed religious
from the existing rules of the Order or abolished
them altogether. Monks and nuns outside the cloister
were already a familiar sight in the fifteenth century,
and in the sixteenth the begging friars obtained
general permission from Rome to live outside their
priories. Community life, and especially community
prayer, fell into disuse. So did voluntary poverty.
Many of the monks retained their inherited estates
and bought or inherited their own cells in the monastery. Erasmus of Rotterdam in his *Enchiridion*
singles out for blame their lovelessness and their
avarice. Other moral transgressions must be added.
The Béguines, for instance, had won for themselves

the nickname of "the Friars' cellaresses". The sister of Duke Magnus was known among the rich Clares of Ribnitz as *impudicissima abbatissa*.

It is not to be wondered at that the "Shaven-heads", as the monks were called, were despised and hated by the people, all the more because they were patently increasing in numbers. Together with the lower clergy and the wandering scholars, the "stormy petrels of the revolution", they formed a clerical proletariat. Johannes Agricola estimated the total number of clergy and religious in Germany at the time—in a small total population—at one million four hundred thousand (Lortz, vol. i, p. 86). It cannot be doubted that the majority of this clerical proletariat had neither the intellectual nor the moral capacity to so much as guess the profundity of the questions raised by Luther, let alone fully to realize the gravity of the challenge and to counter it with an adequate response.

*Omne malum a clero*—every evil comes from the clergy. As early as 1245 at the Council of Lyons, Pope Innocent IV had called the sins of the higher and lower clergy one of the five wounds in the Body of the Church, and at the second Council of Lyons in 1274 Gregory X declared that the wickedness of many prelates was the cause of the ruin of the whole world (cf. Bihlmeyer, vol. ii, p. 336). Machiavelli, again, speaks volumes in the sarcastic remark that

22

"We Italians may thank the Church and our priests that we have become irreligious and wicked" (Lortz, vol. i, p. 119).

In this waste of clerical corruption it was impossible for the spirit of our Lord to penetrate into the people, take root there and bring true religion to flower. Since there was at this time no catechism of infants, the sermons on Sundays and feast-days were the chief sources from which the laity drew their religious education. And these sources were often choked up. Since at this time, moreover, as during the whole of the Middle Ages, Communion was very infrequent outside the ranks of the mystics, there was no sacramental impulse towards an interiorizing and deepening of religion. So the attention of the faithful was directed towards externals. Religion was materialized. Pious interest was focused more on the "holy things"—relics—than on the sacraments, more on pilgrimages and flagellations than on attending the services of the Church, and most of all on indulgences.

The cult of relics and indulgences had grown to gigantic proportions since Leo X had attached indulgences of a thousand, ten thousand and a hundred thousand years to the veneration of relics. Erasmus criticized this kind of piety in the bitter words: "We kiss the shoes of the saints and their dirty kerchiefs while we leave their writings, their holiest and truest

23

relics, to lie unread" (Lortz, vol. i, p. 108). Frederick the Wise, the famous protector of Luther, had built up his treasury of relics in the Castle Church at Wittenburg to 18,885 fragments. Anyone who believed in and venerated them could gain indulgences amounting to two million years. When Boniface IX made of ecclesiastical indulgences what looked like a commercial traffic, even secular princes and cities became eager to take part in the distribution of them, so as to assure for themselves a generous share of the inflowing money.[1]

From the middle of the fifteenth century the Popes began to distribute indulgences for the dead. The Legate Peraudi, in connection with an indulgence granted by Pope Sixtus IV to Louis XI for the whole of France, announces that the indulgence could be made *certainly* effective for any soul in purgatory, even if the person gaining it were in a state of mortal sin, so long as the indulgenced work (i.e., money payment) were performed. Pope Sixtus IV did indeed correct his legate's declaration to the extent of saying that the application of the indulgence to the dead could only be a matter of *petition*, not of

[1] The Jubilee Indulgence of 1390 was extended to various cities besides Rome. A condition for gaining it was a money payment, collected by bankers appointed in the different towns who retained half the sum collected as a commission. See Vansteenberghe, article " Boniface IX " in the *Dictionnaire d' histoire et de géographie ecclésiastique*, vol. ix (1937), p. 919. (Trans.)

24

WEAKNESS IN THE CHURCH

certainty. But Peraudi's other statement—that the indulgence could be gained for the dead by people living in mortal sin—was never censured. In the prevailing low state of clerical education, preachers of the indulgence (such as the Dominican Tetzel for instance) eagerly seized on Peraudi's pronouncement, so that many preachers really did adopt as their favourite tag: "Your cash no sooner clinks in the bowl than out of purgatory jumps the soul." Some of the papal decrees themselves were in great measure responsible for this crude interpretation of indulgences. They employed a misleading formula current from the thirteenth century onwards which spoke of a *remissio a poena et culpa* (remission of pain and guilt) or even of a *remissio peccatorum* (remission of sins),[1] whereas an indulgence is not concerned with the forgiveness of the guilt of sin, nor with the remission of eternal punishment, but only with the remission of temporal punishment, that is, a mitigation or shortening of that penitential suffering which the sinner must undergo either here or in purgatory.

It is unnecessary to emphasize how much this hideous simoniacal abuse of indulgences corrupted

---

[1] These phrases were intended to refer, not only to the indulgence, but to the repentance and absolution that went before it as well. But from the jubilee of 1390 onwards confessors and preachers of indulgences often failed entirely to refer to the necessity of repentance. See Vansteenberghe, loc. cit. (Trans.)

true piety, and how indulgences were perverted to a blasphemous haggling with God. Night fell on the German Church, a night that grew ever deeper and darker as other abuses attached themselves to the excessive cult of relics and the practice of indulgences. The latter was encouraged by the current mass-pilgrimages which were positively epidemic. Associated with them, especially at the time of the Great Schism, was the movement of the flagellants, in which pilgrimage was combined with public self-scourging. Though condemned alike by Pope Clement VI and the Council of Constance they constantly reasserted themselves, uprooted the faithful from their proper situation in parochial and domestic life, and threw them into a state of hysterical excess and unhealthy mysticism.

Behind all these excesses was the driving power of rampant superstition. Allying itself with religion, it had taken possession of the broad mass of the people. It is probably true to say that this superstition had made itself even more at home in the German soul than elsewhere, and developed, even amongst educated people, a vast obsession with the devil. It was a lingering heritage from Germanic and Roman paganism. Since the Inquisition's campaign against the Catharists, who had acknowledged Evil as a first principle, this devil-obsession had begun to ruin daily living and social intercourse. In particular, there was a totally uncritical acceptance of every kind of improbable horror charged against witches. The witch-trials and witch-burnings went on—by inquisitors, secular governments, the reformers (Luther himself taught that witches must be destroyed): and the official Church did not shield the victims of these atrocities with the bulwark of clear Gospel teaching. On the contrary, Innocent VIII, in his Bull *Summis desiderantes* (1484), gave the Dominicans in Constance plenary powers in the matter of witch-burning, and threatened with ecclesiastical punishments anyone who opposed the prosecution of witches. He thus did all that the highest ecclesiastical authority could do to encourage and legalize the obsession. Christ had healed those possessed by devils, but now, in the name of the same Christ, they were to be burnt.

It was night indeed in a great part of Christendom. Such is the conclusion of our survey of the end of the fifteenth century: amongst the common people, a fearful decline of true piety into religious materialism and morbid hysteria; amongst the clergy, both lower and higher, widespread worldliness and neglect of duty; and amongst the very Shepherds of the Church, demonic ambition and sacrilegious perversion of holy things. Both clergy and people must cry *mea culpa, mea maxima culpa!*

Yes, it was night. Had Martin Luther then arisen

27

with his marvellous gifts of mind and heart, his warm penetration of the essence of Christianity, his passionate defiance of all unholiness and ungodliness, the elemental fury of his religious experience, his surging, soul-shattering power of speech, and not least that heroism in the face of death with which he defied the powers of this world—had he brought all these magnificent qualities to the removal of the abuses of the time and the cleansing of God's garden from weeds, had he remained a faithful member of his Church, humble and simple, sincere and pure, then indeed we should to-day be his grateful debtors. He would be forever our great Reformer, our true man of God, our teacher and leader, comparable to Thomas Aquinas and Francis of Assisi. He would have been the greatest saint of the German people, the refounder of the Church in Germany, a second Boniface . . .

But—and here lies the tragedy of the Reformation and of German Christianity—he let the warring spirits drive him to overthrow not merely the abuses in the Church, but the Church Herself, founded upon Peter, bearing through the centuries the *successio apostolica*; he let them drive him to commit what St. Augustine calls the greatest sin with which a Christian can burden himself: he set up altar against altar and tore in pieces the one Body of Christ.

How did this come about? And must we continue for ever to join in that lament of contemporary Christendom which St. Augustine sounded in his work against the Donatists, *Ego laceror valde* (cruelly am I torn)? These are questions which I shall seek to answer.

## II

## LUTHER

WHEN WE pass in review these abuses in the government and people of the Church, the conviction is borne in upon us that everything points to an imminent storm. The angry clamour for a reform in Head and members could be silenced no longer.

But to speak of a *reform of the Head* was an unmistakable indication that people in Germany were not thinking of discarding the Head of the Church, but of improving him. Apart from a few groups of radical humanists and sectarians, the universal detestation was not for the Pope as the divinely instituted guarantee of the Church's unity, not for the religious authority of the Papal See, but only for the utter worldliness of the Popes and the Curia. The desire of all was to have at Rome a real representative of Christ, breathing the spirit of Christ in his person and activity.

And when speaking of a reform of the members, no one thought for a moment of revolutionary changes in the nature of the Church. There was no desire to alter the substance of dogma, cult or ecclesiastical government, only to abolish all the obvious aberrations and distortions of the Church's inner life and devotion. If we avoid being distracted by merely incidental phenomena, and fix our attention on the whole climate of opinion which determined the spirit of the time, we see that the cry for reform was not anti-papal in any dogmatic sense, nor anti-ecclesiastical.

It was a simple, elementary cry for conversion, for total renewal. The conviction had penetrated to the lowest levels of the Christian community that this state of affairs could not go on, that the very heart of the Church was disordered, that, one way or another, a re-formation must come. One way or another! As soon as the possibility was admitted that the change might come some *other* way than that which loyalty to the Church would demand, rebellious and threatening voices mingled with the chorus of the reformers, voices which announced, in the manner of Joachim of Flora, the approach of an apocalyptic visitation and the violent overthrow of all things.

But all these voices went unheard. The Lateran Council of 1513 might energetically deplore the evil state of the Church in Head and members, but a really effective will to reform was lacking. In the next body of cardinals to be created, those who were to be confronted by the Lutheran movement, it was still the prince-prelates of the Renaissance who dominated the picture (Lortz, vol. i, p. 193), not determined men of reforming spirit. And amongst the Popes of the succeeding period, except for Adrian VI, from Clement VII until we arrive at Pius V, there was not one who seriously considered a reform in Head and members. What·followed was therefore inevitable. Instead of a reform there was a revolution, a radical change in the fundamental substance of the Church and Christianity.

## The Final Break

The man who kindled the revolution and pushed on relentlessly towards a final break with the Church was Martin Luther. He was not merely the creator and head of the new movement. He *was* that movement. For that which the Protestant confessions of to-day have in common—what we call to-day the "material principle" of Protestantism, its dogma of the exclusive activity of God and salvation by faith alone, and what we call its "formal principle", its acknowledgment of no other authority than that of Holy Writ—grew out of Luther's whole personal experience and is in its deepest origins his own personal invention. However much Luther may have resisted the dubbing of his own followers "Lutherans", Protestantism is nevertheless in its fundamental substance Lutheran through and through, Luther himself extended and developed.

How did Luther arrive at his new gospel?

The abuses in the Church were not the real *cause* but only the *occasion* of the Reformation. They found their culmination in the shameful deal in indulgences between the Hohenzollern Prince Albert of Brandenburg, the Archbishop of Magdeburg and Mainz and the Papal Curia.[1] The preaching of the special indulgence for the building of St. Peter's was allowed by the Archbishop of Magdeburg and Mainz in his dioceses only on condition that the net profit was to be halved between himself and the fund for St. Peter's. The Archbishop made an arrangement with the great German banking family, the Fuggers, whereby they collected the money. He thus repaid them the sums advanced to him to cover his fees to the Curia for his appointment to the See of Mainz and for the privilege of retaining the Sees of Halberstadt and Magdeburg contrary to Canon Law. Undoubtedly such abuses aroused Luther to the point of coming forward publicly. They explain too why it was that the theses he nailed to the door of the Castle Church at Wittenburg, *De Virtute Indulgentiarum* (concerning the power of indulgences), unleashed such tremendous forces in the German

---

[1] See Philip Hughes, *A History of the Church*, vol. iii, pp. 501–2. (Trans.)

people. Most important of all, they made it possible for Luther to put the Church in the wrong and to justify his own doctrine as the one gospel of salvation before the mass of the people and before his own conscience. Indeed, the longer the strife continued, the more violent became the clash of spirits, the more passionately Luther's hatred of the Pope's Church flamed up; and as he grew older, the confusion in his eyes between the abuses in the Church and the essence of the Church increased, his belief in himself and his mission deepened, and he developed an ever more convinced and more triumphant assurance that he was being summoned by God to overthrow Antichrist in the shape of the Pope.

Thus the abuses within the medieval Church certainly unleashed Luther upon the path of revolution, and justified him in the eyes of the masses and in his own judgment. But they were not the actual ground, the decisive reason for Luther's falling away from the doctrine of the Church. He himself, even, later emphasized that one should not condemn a man's teaching "merely because of his sinful life". "That is not the Holy Spirit. For the Holy Spirit condemns false doctrine and is patient with the weak in faith, as is taught in Romans xiv. 15, and everywhere in Paul. I would have little against the Papists if they taught true doctrine. Their

34

evil life would do no great harm." (Lortz, vol. i, p. 390.)

It was not ecclesiastical abuses that made him the opponent of the Catholic Church, but the conviction that she was *teaching* falsely. And this conviction dates from long before the fatal 17th October, 1517. He had interiorly abandoned the teaching of the Church long before he outwardly raised the standard of revolt. Certainly, as early as 1512, without as yet knowing or wishing it, he had grown away from the Church's belief (Lortz, vol. i, p. 191). How did this come about? In asking this question, we are confronted by the mystery of Luther, by the problem of his whole personal development.

## The Mystery of Luther

In reaching a judgment on his development it is necessary to remember that Luther, doubtless very strictly brought up in his father's house at Eisleben, was early imbued with a strong central experience of fear, an extraordinary terror of sin and judgment. This alone accounts for the fact that when he was caught in a thunderstorm near Stotternheim and nearly struck by lightning he cried out: "Help me, Saint Anne! I will become a monk." He was overcome by a similar spiritual crisis at his first Mass. It was so violent that he almost had to leave the celebration unfinished. It is also significant that once, when at the conventual Mass the Gospel of the man possessed by the devil was being read, he cried out: "It is not I!" and fell down like a dead man (Lortz, vol. i, p. 161, n.).

These accesses of terror betray an unusual degree of sensitivity, stimulated by his deeply rooted fear in the face of the *tremendum mysterium* of God, which for him reached its most shattering clarity in the Crucifixion of the Son of God. Since his attitude to life was determined at its very roots by this fear, Luther was radically subjectivist. That is to say, he was naturally inclined to take into the tension of his own subjective consciousness all objective truths and values presented to him from without, and only then to evaluate their importance and significance. If any truth or value could not be thus assimilated to the thoughts already in the depths of his fearful soul, he had no great interest in it. Thus his religious thought was from the start eclectic, one-sidedly selective. From the start it was thought overcharged with feeling, enveloped by a secret fear and labouring under the tormenting question: how am I to find a merciful God? From the start the primary object of his thought was to release the tension in his own soul, to deliver himself, to bring tranquillity to his distraught spirit. Always the stress was on *I*, everything pivoting on his own experience. On the other hand, it cannot be doubted, in face of Luther's tremendous achievements in thought, decision and action, that despite this tension he was psychically healthy to the core. In everything that he thought, preached and wrote Luther betrays a robust vitality, an overflowing energy, an inexhaustible originality, an elemental creative power which raised him far above the level of common humanity.

With these predispositions, Luther entered the priory of barefooted Augustinians at Erfurt, probably against his father's will. Here he was to prepare himself, by strict spiritual discipline and hard study, for his future entry into the Order and the priesthood. The system of thought, the form in which all philosophical knowledge was then presented, both in the priory and in the neighbouring University of Wittenberg, was the "new way" of Scotism, with the stamp of its later Ockhamist development. Ockhamism had a decisive influence on Luther. He described himself as a member of the Ockhamist school (*sum occamicae factionis*). More precisely, he counted himself a Gabrielist, i.e., a follower of the Tübingen theologian Gabriel Biel, who had adapted Ockhamism, bringing it more into line with the teaching of the Church.

From Ockhamism Luther received his anti-metaphysical tendencies, his dislike of the Aristotelian and Scholastic doctrine founded on the objective validity of universal concepts. From Ockham too he took his concept of God. God is God precisely because of His absolute, unconditioned will, His sovereign freedom and dominion, which is beyond any scale of values and by whose arbitrary choice alone this order of values was created. God is a God of arbitrary choice. He can therefore predestine some in advance to eternal salvation, others in advance to eternal damnation.

Particularly important for Luther's inner development is the Ockhamist doctrine of justification. Pre-Lutheran Thomism, the Church's classical doctrine of grace, presents grace as a movement of divine love entering into the penitent soul and delivering it from the bonds of its fallen nature. In contrast with this, grace in Ockhamism remains strictly transcendent. Justification consists solely in a *relatio externa*, a new relationship of mercy between man and God established by God's love, by means of which all a man's religious and moral acts, *though remaining in themselves human and natural*, are accounted as salvific acts in the eyes of a merciful God. In Ockhamism, it is true, justification is still God's work of grace, in so far as human activity only becomes salvific by God's recognition of it, by His act of acceptance. But this recognition and validation does not in any way affect man's spiritual powers. It remains completely outside him and is simply seen and assented to by faith. Thus for

practical purposes on the psychological plane it is
as though nothing were involved but purely human
activity, and as if devotion were only a matter of
human acts.

Thus the intellectual situation in which Luther
found himself was insecure and threatened on all
sides. Natural reality was not a harmony of truths
and values, accessible to knowledge and fundamentally intelligible, but an ultimately unknowable
multiplicity of concrete singulars, a world of confusion and riddles. And supernatural reality, the
living God of revelation, is a hidden God (*deus
absconditus*), far removed from any kind of tie, sheer
creative omnipotence to which we are completely
delivered up. There is but one way of escape from
this overwhelming combined threat from above and
below: blind fulfilment of the arbitrary commands
of this arbitrary God as they are shown to us in
revelation, the way of good works. It is a way
crowded at each moment with moral activity, but
for this very reason a perilous way, a way of
stumbling and falling.

It is easy to see that the perilous and menacing
situation thus resulting from the ideas of Ockhamism
was bound to have a seriously disturbing effect on a
religious sensibility already as troubled with fear as
Luther's. The consequence was a series of crises,
struggles and temptations. The readings from the

Bible and from the writings of St. Augustine upon which his Order laid particular stress again helped to increase Luther's religious terror. It was in fact St. Augustine who, in his disputes with the Semi-Pelagians, pushed the Biblical doctrine of predestination to the furthest extreme, going so far as to speak of a "reprobate mass" from which only a few just would be chosen. Luther's first years in the priory were thus a time of interior tension, spiritual struggle and suffering. The hopeless feeling that he was not numbered among the elect but among the reprobate overcame him and grew stronger as he grew more and more conscious that he did not fulfil God's commandments in all things. Since he began early to condemn as sin every movement of natural appetite, even though unwilling, and since, with his exuberant vitality, such movements kept recurring, he supposed himself to be full of sin, and no prayer, fasting or confession could free him of this terror.

For many years Luther was thus visited by scruples. "I know a man who believes that he has often experienced the pains of Hell" (Lortz, vol. i, p. 174), a sign of the seriousness with which he regarded his vocation as a Christian and a religious, and on the other hand an indication of how far Ockhamism had obscured the Christian gospel of grace. The strange and tragic thing in Luther's development

40

was that, in his Ockhamist aversion from all meta-physics and especially from the "old way" of Scholasticism, he remained closed to the traditional Catholic doctrine of grace as represented by the great masters of Scholasticism, Albert the Great, Thomas Aquinas and Bonaventure. It suffered indeed a temporary decline in the late Middle Ages, but was taken up again by the "Prince of Thomists" Johannes Capreolus and re-established in all its ancient purity by Luther's contemporary, Cardinal Cajetan. Ockhamist optimism, in fact, in its practical, living results, bordered close on the Pelagian denial of Original Sin.

In contrast to this the Catholic teaching sets fallen man, man burdened with Original Sin and its consequences, in the centre of the divine plan of salvation. It does not present salvation as a pronouncement by God's free graciousness of the justice of our purely human efforts to reach the redemptive riches of Christ. Salvation consists on the contrary in the grace and love of Christ, merited by the sacrifice of the Cross and penetrating fallen man, constantly washing away our guilt and supplying for our weakness by the sacraments and awakening us to new life in Christ. The fundamental attitude of redeemed man, according to the Church's doctrine, is thus not the fear of sin and terror of damnation but trusting faith in the grace of Christ, which constantly snatches us away from all guilt and gives us Christ for our own.

If Luther had entrusted himself to this traditional Catholic doctrine of Grace, which his friend Johann von Staupitz, the Augustinian Provincial, constantly laid before him, he would not have had that experience in the tower which laid the foundation for his abandonment of the doctrine of the Church.

## The Doctrine of Justification

Luther describes this experience in 1545, one year before his death—fairly late, in fact. His other recollections were also made late in life, and contain a number of "foreshortenings" of various kinds (Lortz, vol. i, p. 178). So it is likely enough that a whole series of thoughts and impressions of a similar kind led up to this decisive experience in the monastery tower at Wittenburg, which was merely the final precipitation of them. In any case, a fundamental departure from the Catholic doctrine of justification is settled once for all in this experience in the tower in 1512.

As Luther himself expressed it, it was concerned with a deeper understanding of the Epistle to the Romans, starting with the Pauline concept of the "justice of God". St. Paul had written: "The justice of God is revealed therein"—i.e., in the Gospel (Rom. i. 17). Hitherto he had not been able to make anything of the scriptural words "the justice of God". "I did not love this just God, the punisher of sins, rather I hated Him." Only after pondering a long while "both day and night" did he perceive that the Apostle of the Gentiles did not mean by the "justice of God" active, judicial, primitive justice, but passive justice, i.e., that by which the merciful God justifies us by faith, as it is written: "The just man liveth by faith." Luther immediately re-examined in this light all the related texts in Holy Scripture which he remembered at the time, and found that they were all to be understood in this sense. "Then truly I felt that I had been born again and had entered through open gates into the highest heaven."

Thus his experience in the tower laid the foundation of Luther's *theology of consolation*: Christianity is pure grace, not the work of man. It is in this sense that he interprets the words of the Apostle (Rom. iii. 28): "For we account a man to be justified by faith, without the works of the law." It is strange that Luther should have considered that this interpretation of the "justice of God" was a completely *new* discovery, differentiating his exegesis from that of "all the doctors". In actual fact practically all the medieval exegetes proposed the same meaning for it. They all took "the justice of God" in the passive sense, as meaning a justice by which we are justified, which makes us just. But they did not draw from this the catastrophic conclusion that Luther drew and which, in his 1515–16 lectures on the Epistle to the Romans, he claimed as the true meaning and content of the Epistle: "In the Epistle to the Romans Paul teaches us the reality of sin in us and the unique justice of Christ."

This is the culminating point of his new discovery: man is sin, nothing but sin. Even the man who is justified remains *peccator*. What justifies him is the sole justice of Christ, imputed to him on the ground of his trusting faith. There is thus no question of the justice of any work of man. Man's part is merely to recognize his sinfulness in true repentance and, in this terror-stricken awareness (*conscientia pavida*), to reach out towards the Cross of Christ. It is God's grace alone which delivers him. As Christ Himself was at once "accursed and blessed", living and dead, suffering and rejoicing, so the believing Christian is at once a sinner and justified. From now on Luther delights in thus putting the inexpressible in the form of a paradox: the believing Christian is at once a sinner and justified, at once condemned and absolved, at once accursed and blessed.

From the psychological point of view, Luther's total denial of any justice in works and his unconditional assent to grace alone constituted an act of self-liberation from the fearful oppression which his moral life had suffered under Ockhamist theology and its exclusive emphasis on the human factor in the process of justification. From now on he resolutely cast himself loose from *all* justice in works, from all human activity, and threw himself upon the justifying grace of Christ, thus getting rid once and for all of all scrupulosity and terror of sin. Now he is spiritually free: free not only from the exaggerations of the Ockhamist School with its over-emphasis on works, but free from *any* form of justice in works, including that which the Catholic Church had always taught; free, as he was later to say, from the *captivitas babylonica*.

He won this freedom through a series of arduous battles and defeats, in hard struggles by day and night. It is this that gives his new experience its inner validity and its tremendous explosive power. If he had attained to this new interpretation of justification by a purely speculative process, as a mere intellectual conclusion, an exegetical discovery, the matter might have rested there. He might have remained unmolested within the Church, since there were other Catholic theologians, of the Augustinian school, teaching something similar, and since no Tridentine dogma had yet authoritatively defined the relation between faith and works, or the process of justification. His new theses would perhaps have been attacked here and there, perhaps have been censured. He might have been regarded as a theological outsider, but he would still have remained a Catholic theologian.

But his expositions were more than mere academic treatises; for him, those ninety-five theses nailed to the door of the Castle Church at Wittenberg mirrored the *Evangelium*, the sole hope of salvation, upon which one could stake one's life; and the source of this feeling is to be found in those nights in the monastery, those hours of fear and agony when he burned with the fierce heat of his struggles for his soul's salvation. His new interpretation of the justice of God was sealed with his heart's blood, born of the dire need of his conscience—and for this reason it was infinitely dear to him. All the defiance of his passionate temperament, all the unrepressed impetuosity of his robust peasant nature, the rich endowments of his mind, his heroic readiness to commit himself to the full, his immense creative power in observation, thought and writing, and not least his wonderful power of speech, beating upon the hearer in climax after climax and "fairly overwhelming him" (Lortz, vol. i, p. 147)—all these powers united now in a tremendous *sense of mission*, a conviction that he, he alone, had rediscovered the Gospel and was called to proclaim it to the whole world. Armed with this sense of mission, which asserted itself ever more strongly and triumphantly as the years went by, he, barefooted Augustinian friar of Wittenberg, went forth against a whole world, against the Christian Middle Ages, against the weight of the world-wide Catholic Church, against Pope and Emperor, and, not the least formidable, against the bronze ring of sacred custom with which men's consciences had for centuries been inextricably bound.

## Christendom Divided

Let me stress it once again: Luther's abandonment of belief in the Church was not a conclusion reached in the cold, clear light of critical thought, but in the heat of religious experience; indeed, his whole development was less a matter of intellectual insights than of emotional impressions. From the sheer intellectual point of view, Luther *never* abandoned the idea of the one true Church. His theological *thought* did not touch on the erection of a new Church, but on the renewal of the old. Even in 1518, when he had to give an account of himself to the Cardinal-Legate Cajetan, he declared: "If any man can show me that I have said anything contrary to the opinion of the holy Roman Church, I will be my own judge, and recant" (Lortz, vol. i, p. 393). And in the *Commentary on a Certain Article* in 1519 he commits himself, entirely according to the

47

mind of St. Augustine, to the principle that one may not "for any sin or evil whatever that man may think or name, sever love and divide spiritual unity, for love can do all things".

But the world of feeling within him had been stirred to its depths; the violence of his experience overwhelmed all these rational considerations. The harder his Catholic opponents pressed him, the more he let himself be swept into a declaration of war against the whole Church. In his ninety-five theses on indulgences he had already questioned the power of the Church over the riches of salvation; in his Leipzig Disputation in 1519 he attacked the infallible authority of General Councils and of the Church's doctrinal tradition and admitted as religious truth only what can be deduced from Holy Scripture.

From 1520 onwards he openly attacked the Pope as Antichrist. His address, *To the Christian Nobility of the German Nation*, which appeared in the same year, was, as Karl Müller expresses it, "a trumpet-call to seize all the possessions of the Papacy". And in his later polemical writing, *De Captivitate Babylonica*, of the Church's seven sacraments he admitted only Baptism, the Lord's Supper, and, partially, Penance, branding the other sacraments, together with the Church's teaching on transubstantiation and the Sacrifice of the Mass, as *captivitas babylonica*, a miserable imprisonment of the faithful. In the work which was the third main statement of the Reformation, *Of the Freedom of a Christian Man,* he portrayed the ideal of Christian life in the light of his new doctrine and sent it to the Pope. In this same year, 1520, as the public expression of his complete abandonment of the Church, he burned the volumes of the Canon Law and the Papal Bull threatening him with excommunication before the Elster Gate of Wittenberg. The Pope's answer was sentence of excommunication.

His break with the Church was complete. He went forward in the midst of a mass-apostasy of princes and cities, secular and regular clergy, nobles and humanists, burghers and peasants. There followed the Protestation of the Lutheran Princes and Cities against the decision of the Reichstag at Speier in 1529, which gave the new religionists the name of "Protestants". And then came the Reichstag at Augsburg in 1530, which, with its rejection of Melanchthon's mediatory *Confessio Augustana,* destroyed the last hope of a reconciliation of minds. Christianity in Germany was divided, and has remained so until this very day.

## The New Rule of Faith

We must first reiterate the fact, admitted by all modern scholars, that Luther's departure from the Church's rule of faith was brought about by a *sub-*

49

*jective* experience—his experience in the tower in 1512. As we have already said, abuses in the Church certainly strengthened Luther in this experience. They certainly armed him with his best weapons against Rome, and accounted to no small extent for the tremendous response of the German nation to his new Gospel. But they did not create this gospel; Luther did not arrive at his new interpretation of the gospel by looking at the deplorable abuses in the Church around him. He arrived at it by looking at the crying need of his own soul, the result of the conflict between the terror of sin which had oppressed him from his youth and the rigorous demands made on him by the Ockhamist doctrine of atonement. He was delivered from these straits by his experience of all-sufficient saving faith, the experience of grace alone.

It was a completely subjective experience arising out of the acute anxiety of his own individual mind, and it was so elemental in character that it not only drew into itself all similar religious impressions and dominated them, but also spread out over all his thinking and compelled him to see and accept only those truths which came in some way within the orbit of this central experience, and to ignore all the truths of Scripture which lay outside it. Only thus can we explain, for instance, his calling the Epistle of St. James, because of its emphasis on the

justice of works, an "epistle of straw". Only thus
can we explain the fact that he does not go in the
first instance to Christ our Lord Himself, speaking
to us in the Gospels, but to the written testimony of
St. Paul, the last of the Apostles to be called, who
was never an eye- or ear-witness of the life of Jesus.
And only thus can we explain his complete failure
to realize what interpretations and rearrangements
need to be made to derive that doctrine of grace
which Luther thought he could find in St. Paul from
the most profound passages of Jesus' own teaching,
the Sermon on the Mount, with its clear theme of
works and rewards.

The subjectivity of his central experience can be
said to have dominated his theology, determining
the special way in which he read and commented
the Bible. It is a theology of subjective selection.
Luther was certainly not a religious individualist in
the ordinary sense, trusting exclusively to the emana-
tions of his own thought and to his own experiences
when dealing with theological issues. On the contrary, his trembling spirit was confronted by the
colossal reality of the God of Revelation, and the
shattering impact of His Gospel. He knew himself
bound to this mightiest of objectives, in the same
way that he continued to accept ancient and medieval
cosmology as final truth. To this extent Luther was,
as Troeltsch puts it (*Collected Writings*, 1922, vol. iv,

p. 286), "a completely conservative revolutionary". The word of revelation laid down in the Bible remained for him the unique source of all religious knowledge. But it was not the objective spirit of the Church's tradition speaking and witnessing in the Church's teaching which interpreted this objective word of revelation, but his *own* spirit alone; not the *We* of the members of Christ inspired by a common faith and love, but his own unique, individual *I*. In this formal, though not material, sense Luther was always a subjectivist.

It is true that this subjectivism arose largely from truly religious depths, rooted, ultimately, in an elementary experience of the uncertainty and the helpless need for salvation of fallen human nature. There could be no greater mistake than to see, in the religious movement which had Luther as its origin, nothing but the product of a completely personal fear-psychosis. Luther's fear is the fear of all of us, the guilty fear of human nature enmeshed in the consequences of Original Sin. This alone explains why the Reformer's experience was, and is, capable of creating a communion. But on the other hand, neither can it be doubted that the special structure of this experience, its depth and comprehensiveness and its theological and sociological developments, bear always those marks of subjectivism which belong to Luther's singular, exceptional spiritual development alone, and are in no way common to humanity.

"Luther's great mistake in constituting his doctrine was that he took his own highly personal convictions, based on a very exceptional experience and perhaps valid for himself personally, and made them into a binding requirement for all" (Lortz, vol. i, p. 408). It was to be expected from the start that this subjectivist basis would be far too narrow and scanty to remain the standard interpretation of Christ for a whole world with its thousands of individual characters. Thus even in Luther's own lifetime divisions arose over essential points. Before his very eyes there took place a certain loosening and weakening of his doctrine, a loosening which left open at least the *possibility* that even the most differing sects might be able to meet each other in discussion.

The scholarly side of Lutheran Christianity, as much as its individual and even individualist origin, offers many things favourable to an understanding with Catholic Christianity. We must, of course, make it clear first that we are not considering the emasculated Christianity produced by the Enlightenment and German Idealist philosophy but *Luther's* Christianity, the original Lutheranism which he himself founded and built up. In a stimulating lecture entitled *What are Catholic Tendencies?* a leading Lutheran Bishop, Wilhelm Stählin of Oldenburg,

has made a determined attack on that modern perversion of Lutheran belief which considers the
"banalities of unbridled liberalism" born of the
Enlightenment as the true essence of Protestantism.
It is an attitude which thinks that the difference
between Protestant and Catholic is simply that the
Protestant "feels that he is only responsible to his
own conscience", so that for him there is "no binding dogma and no compulsory creed", or at any
rate, that he "pushes certain aspects of the Bible
message out of sight or at least to the very edge of
his field of vision". Anyone who speaks of the
binding nature of a dogma, of the presence of Christ
in the cult of the Church or of a necessary ecclesiastical order is at once—so Stählin complains—
accused of Catholic tendencies. In fact, he says with
emphasis, dogma, cult and the Church's constitution
belong to the *"true heritage* of the Reformation".
And in reality it was "a sign of decline, a morbid
symptom" when these ordinances were set aside in
the name of the individual conscience. "If a man
believes," Stählin goes on to say, "that he can
sacrifice the fullness of the Christian revelation to
some vague formless religious feeling or vague belief
in Providence, he may hold himself to be a good
Protestant, but in the true Reformation sense of the
word, he is simply not a Christian."

To some extent this condemnation of Stählin's

falls also on a type of Lutheran theology and a mental attitude which regards the liberation of the individual's conscience from despair as the essence of Christianity, and entirely ignores the sacramental *framework* in which this conscience has its roots, the holy ordinances of the Church. Of such a Protestantism it is true to say what Nietzsche believed to be true of Protestantism in general—that it was "a one-sided laming" of Christianity (*Antichrist*, viii, 225).

Luther himself did not leave the matter in doubt; for him the Confession of Augsburg in 1530 was compulsory doctrine, acknowledgment of which was a condition of membership of the Church (cf. Loofs, *History of Dogma*, 4th ed., p. 748). So we are confronted, in Lutheran Christianity, with the recognition of an *objective ecclesiastical teaching authority*, with which every individual Christian conscience must come to terms. It is true that the Protestant conscience is more loosely bound to this authority than a Catholic's is, because the authority does not, as in the Catholic Church, rest upon the visible rock of Peter and is not visibly guaranteed by the apostolic succession of bishops. Looking at it closely, the Protestant conscience is bound to the collective mind of the Church as a whole, not to those visible authorities in particular who are the bearers and sustainers of that collective mind. Nevertheless, in

Lutheranism too, Christian consciences are not simply sovereign, but obliged to submit to the teaching voice of their Church.

Indeed we might go further, and say that though Protestant consciences may be more loosely bound, the tie is not *essentially* any different from that binding the Catholic. For the Catholic, too, it is not ultimately the objective norm of the teaching voice but the subjective decision of *conscience* which has finally to decide on a believing acceptance of the revealed truth laid down by the authority of the Church. It is really not the case that the faith of a Catholic is entirely accounted for by slavish obedience to the rigid law of the Church. He, too, is making a personal act, an act of reflective thought and moral decision springing from the deep centre of his freedom, an act of choice. For him too it is an act that can only be performed in the conscience itself. Indeed, if his conscience, on subjectively cogent grounds, becomes involved in invincible error and he finds himself compelled to refuse his assent to the Church's teaching, he is, in the Catholic view, bound to leave the Church. The most eminent of Catholic theologians, St. Thomas Aquinas, expressly declares that a man is bound in conscience to separate himself from the Christian body if he is unable to believe in the divinity of Christ.[1] Thus

[1] *Summa Theologica*, I–II, 19, 5.

the two confessions meet each other both in their recognition of an ecclesiastical teaching authority and in the decisive place they give to the judgment of the individual conscience.

Furthermore, in their attitude to the Sacred Scriptures they are not nearly so opposed to each other as might appear from the formal Lutheran principle of "the Scripture alone". The Catholic Church re-affirmed and reformulated in the Councils of Trent and of the Vatican the ancient truth of the Christian faith that Scripture is inspired by the Holy Ghost, whereas modern Protestant theology tends more and more to admit only Revelation, not Scripture, as inspired, the bearers of the Revelation being themselves enlightened by the Holy Ghost, but not their writings. So that one can say that the authority of Holy Scripture is fundamentally better safeguarded and more strongly emphasized in Catholicism than in Protestantism.

Because they are inspired by the Holy Ghost, the Scriptures, and especially the New Testament, are always, for the Catholic too, the classical source of Christianity. They present, so to speak, the conscious mind of the Church. But the Catholic is convinced that the Church has also what might be called a subconscious mind. It consists of those remembrances, ordinances and traditions of primitive Christianity received directly from Christ but handed on only *orally* by the Apostles, which were not expressly formulated in Holy Scripture, although in the strictest sense they embody a primitive Christian deposit of faith. This extra-Biblical stream of tradition must have existed from the beginning, since the first disciples, like their Divine Master, at first spread the Good News only orally, and it was by oral teaching alone that they aroused the faith of the first Christian communities. When they wrote the Gospels and Epistles, they already took for granted the existence of a living Christianity in the various communities, as the writings themselves show.

Nor is it of course the case that the Apostles and Evangelists were trying to achieve in their writings a comprehensive, exhaustive survey of the Christian message, a sort of early catechism. It would be hard even to-day to piece together a single, unselfcontradictory system of thought from the Bible without reference to the oral tradition. The aim of the Apostles and Evangelists was rather to *inspire* and *deepen* the religion of the Christian communities, always according to the different circumstances in which they wrote and with reference to the growing problems which they encountered—not in any true sense to *establish* it. Thus not all the Apostles wrote; and again several of St. Paul's Epistles are lost to us. What brought the Christian communities to life in the first place was *oral preaching,* not the Scriptures.

Again, we only know of the very existence of the Scriptures, and of what is included in them, by oral tradition. To this extent their authority is ultimately dependent upon that of the Church's teaching.

In the light of this overwhelming importance attaching to the Church's tradition, the Lutheran scriptural principle cannot any longer be upheld in its original form. On the other hand, we must remark on the Catholic side a reawakening of interest in the Bible, which has not only affected professional theologians but has become a widespread movement among the common people of the Church. Nor is there any lack of voices acknowledging Luther's translation of the Bible, with its vigorous language tingling with the violence of religious experience, as a classical example worthy of emulation.

It cannot be over-emphasized that those truths which are uniquely Christian, distinguishing Christianity from all other religions: the mysteries of the Three-Personed God, of the Son of God made man, of our redemption by the Cross, of the sanctification of the faithful by Baptism, Penance and Eucharist, of the coming of the Judge of all the world, of the Last Things—it is just this ground-plan and *centre* of the Christian message which forms the core of *both* our Christian confessions. Will it not be possible to find paths radiating from this centre which will bring us to unity in those things which are less central? What divides us is not so much *what* we believe as the various different ways in which we take into ourselves and realize this one gift of Faith —problems about the nature of saving faith, the process of justification, the relation between faith and sacrament, the teaching, pastoral and priestly office of the Church. These are certainly matters of importance, and, for the sake of revealed truth, we cannot neutralize them or indeed yield anything concerning them. But they are nevertheless questions which would not, in the light of *early* Lutheran piety, be so involved and utterly insoluble as would appear from the religious situation to-day.

We must consider, for example, the fact that Confession and the honouring of the Blessed Virgin— two forms of devotion which a modern Protestant condemns as specifically Catholic—occupied an important position in Luther's own devotional life. Right up to his death he paid homage in his sermons to the Mother of God; right up to his death he went to confession to his friend Bugenhagen. "I should long ago have been strangled by the Devil," he acknowledges, "if I had not been upheld by private confession." It was the orthodox Lutheran theology of the seventeenth and eighteenth centuries that eliminated devotion to Mary and Confession from Protestant practice.

We should be even more struck by the fact that the

"Confession of Augsburg" (*Confessio Augustana*), drawn up by Melanchthon and approved by Luther, which in evangelical Christianity ranks even to-day as an authoritative confession of faith, makes no mention in its first part of any fundamental dogmatic difference, not even of the primacy of the Pope or indulgences, and in fact expressly declares that the whole dispute is concerned only with certain *abuses* (*tota dissensio est de paucis quibusdam abusibus*). And in the second part, where it enumerates these abuses, it names simply: Communion under one kind, celibacy, private Masses (i.e., the current commercial traffic in hole-and-corner Masses), compulsory confession, the laws of fasting, monastic vows and the abuse of episcopal authority; in other words, only things which in the Catholic view do not belong to the unalterable *regula fidei,* the sphere of faith, but to the *regula disciplinae,* the sphere of ecclesiastical discipline, which the Church could, if she saw fit, alter.

And even these abuses, as Melanchthon notes them, take on their repulsive, scandalous aspect only against the background of late medieval practice. Celibacy, monastic vows, compulsory confession and the so-called commercial hole-and-corner Masses had been perverted from the glorious truth that underlay them. These detestable perversions will never return. The reforming Council of Trent tore them up by the roots. The evangelical historian Karl August Meissinger made some significant remarks in this connection in his essay on "Luther's Day": "If Luther returned to-day . . . he would find to his astonishment a Roman Church which he would never have attacked in her present aspect . . . Above all he would see . . . that not one of the abuses which were the actual occasion of his break with Rome remains in existence."

It is true that Melanchthon, starting from his urgent wish for an understanding, seems to have been too optimistic when he spoke in the Confession simply of "certain abuses" which must be removed. For it cannot be doubted that Luther regarded some at least of his objections as fundamental. But here too we must not overlook the fact that in taking up this radical position he still started from the abuses within the Church, and that ultimately it was his total opposition, born of his deep religious experience, to everything unholy, together with his volcanic impetuosity, which led him to make a clean sweep, to be done completely with all these abuses, and then to provide his destructive beginnings with a theoretical basis.

## Salvation by Faith Alone

We have already shown how even his principal doctrine of salvation by faith alone is largely accounted for by his resentment against the stress laid by Ockhamism on the human factor in justification. Since he was insufficiently acquainted with the great masters of Scholasticism, he simply identified the radically un-Catholic Ockhamist doctrine of justification with the teaching of the Catholic Church. When we look into it we see that his phrase "faith alone" is directly aimed only against the Ockhamist supposition that a man, once he is called to salvation by God's grace, can and must work out his own salvation by his own power and his own self-mastery. It was aimed, then, against the Pelagianism lurking in the Ockhamist doctrine of justification, which made salvation dependent solely on human power. But it was not directly aimed against that other supposition, that man can and must work out his salvation *by the power of Christ,* that all human choice and action only becomes salvific when it is caught up by the grace of Christ. It is a cleavage of ideas going right through to the heart of our conception of God: whether man is to be thought of as a completely autonomous, independent co-operator —or, if he wishes, opponent—of God in the scheme of redemption, or simply as passive in His hand, unable to work out his salvation except in grace and through grace. It is the latter which has always been the clear, unambiguous teaching of the Catholic Church. It was first actually formulated at the Second

Council of Orange in 529 against the Semi-Pelagians, and repeated at Trent, illuminated by our Lord's image of the branch which can only flourish and bring forth fruit in the vine. Looking at it truly and profoundly, it was not against *this* that Luther raged and fought. His doctrine of faith and grace alone would have had its right place, its true significance, within the framework of Catholic dogma; so long as he meant by "faith alone" that faith which is active through love.

In fact, the phrase "salvation by faith alone" has never been alien to Catholic theology. It was in fact always Catholic teaching that we can only be saved by Christ alone, that it is only God's unmerited, unmeritable grace that lifts us out of the state of sin and death into that of divine sonship, and that even the so-called "meritorious acts" which the redeemed perform in a state of justice are only "meritorious by grace", attributable, that is, to the love of Christ working in us and through us. In so far as the justification of man is God's work alone, we could speak with Luther of "extrinsic" justice. It is indeed also interior and personal. Luther too, in that same commentary on the Epistle to the Romans, affirms that this extrinsic justice "dwells in us by faith and hope", that it is "in us" though it does not belong to us (*in nobis est, non nostra*), that it thus, according to the Council of Trent, "inheres" in justified man (*atque ipsis inhaeret*, sess. 6, cap. 7, can. 11).

In the same way Luther's other doctrine, that the justified man is at once a sinner and just (*simul peccator et justus*), can bear a Catholic interpretation if we do not take it theologically but psychologically, if we regard justification not from God's point of view but from man's. In the first case it is indeed always a matter of Yes *or* No, election or reprobation, but in the second, it is a question of Yes *and* No, in so far as our hardest striving is always accompanied by some secret attachment to sin (cf. R. Grosche, *Pilgernde Kirche*, 1938, pp. 150 ff.). The Catholic too must pray day by day "forgive us our trespasses". Throughout his liturgy echoes the cry: "Lord, have mercy on us. Regard not my sins! Give us peace!" Even when the justified soul is no longer in a state of sin, it is still sinful. Every serious Catholic will wish and have to pray with St. Thérèse of the Child Jesus: ". . . I do not ask You to count my good works, Lord. All our justice is full of imperfection in Your eyes. So I will clothe myself in Your justice and receive from Your love eternal possession of Yourself."

It was the Thomistic school itself which anticipated Luther's pessimistic view of humanity, since it taught that the capacity of fallen man to receive God's action is purely passive, which grace alone can arouse to activity and freedom. We can affirm absolutely that Luther's battle, fundamentally and essentially, was only with the Ockhamist perversion of the Catholic doctrine of justification, with an abuse within the Church, as Melanchthon rightly saw, an abuse which was never accepted by the Church. Ockham himself was arraigned before a court of the Holy Office at Avignon[1] and kept in custody, until he fled to the protection of Ludwig of Bavaria; though the fact that the subsequent spread of his doctrine was tolerated gave the hot-blooded Reformer a seeming justification in identifying Ockhamism with Catholicism and in denying, along with the abuse itself, its primitive Christian and Catholic background.

*Priesthood and Sacraments*

A similar reaction against public abuses within the Church accounts for Luther's radical discarding of the seven sacraments and the separate priesthood. In his polemic *De Captivitate Babylonica* he expressly speaks of the multitude of human regulations with which the Church had made of the sacraments a miserable captivity for the faithful.

His own master, Gabriel Biel, had taught him, entirely in accordance with the Catholic interpretation, that in the Mass there is no question of a fresh

[1] But *not* for his teaching on justification. (Trans.)

immolation of Christ, but only of a ritual re-presenta-
tion of the one sacrifice of Golgotha, and thus that
through the Mass the one sacrifice of Christ is
brought out of the past into our present moment,
into our Here and Now. Nevertheless Luther's
violent rejection of the sacrifice of the Mass can
only be understood in relation to that crude external-
ization, secularization even, which had penetrated
even to the innermost sanctuary of the Church and,
as Luther complained, made "the Altar of the All
Highest into an altar of Baal" (Lortz, vol. i, p. 399).
When the clergy were not paid sufficiently for saying
Mass they used to say a *missa sicca*, i.e., they broke
off the Mass before the Consecration. And when the
faithful had a Mass said for them they often saw in
it not so much the memorial of the death of the Lord
as a kind of magic protecting them from earthly
harm. As in the former case, Luther here identified
a vulgar perversion of current practice with Catholicism itself, and made a clean sweep, rejecting the
Mass as sacrifice and accepting only the Supper.

As the logical consequence of all this, Luther
rejected along with the sacraments those who dispensed them; he would have nothing of an official
priesthood. It is true that his view of the priesthood
of the laity was directly in line with his key-doctrine
of salvation by faith alone. But it was not in fact
because of such speculative theological considera-

tions that he adopted this line and pursued it—he was not speculatively inclined, it was the rage of the reformer, wounded in his deepest religious sensibilities by the frightful degradation of the secular and regular clergy, that convinced him that the priesthood and the religious state were in themselves the origin and the bulwark of abuse, and that they must therefore be torn up by the roots.

But precisely because it was the abuses in the sacramental life that Luther had before his eyes, he never intended to attack the essence of the sacraments themselves, the idea of the sacraments in the Church. In other words, he did not mean to undermine the belief that heavenly gifts are exhibited to us and imparted to us in simple, earthly symbols. His confidence in the objective efficacy of the sacraments is all the more striking in that the subjectivity of his belief concerning salvation must have exerted pressure on him in the opposite direction. And yet he clung to their objective efficacy. He made it clear that he believed that the miracle of grace by which saving faith is imparted is performed in the act of Baptism itself. For this reason he accepted infant Baptism from the Church's tradition, although infants cannot have trusting faith.

Similarly, in deliberate opposition to the "Sacramentarians", as he called Zwingli's followers, he associated the presence of the glorified Christ with the elements of the Eucharist; not, that is, directly with the subjective faith of the person receiving the Sacrament but with the objective faith of the Church, acknowledging the presence of Christ in these elements. When Luther, in his dispute with the Swiss Protestants, expressly taught that even those who are personally unbelieving or unworthy receive the very Body of the Lord, he was testifying in the clearest way to the ancient Catholic belief in the physical as well as spiritual presence of our glorified Lord. It is something independent of the faith within the soul of the communicant.

By retaining the Church's Sacrament of Penance —though without the obligation to confess and without the performance of satisfaction—by separating repentance from justification and holding that justification was only completed in the act of receiving the Sacrament, he was again giving decisive importance not to the trusting faith of the person alone but also to the extra-personal, impersonal outward sign. Thus a roundabout way was opened for the reintroduction of a kind of Sacrament of Penance, and as Harnack sarcastically says: "A practice was created which was even worse, because laxer, than the Roman confessional" (*History of Dogma,* 6th ed., p. 472).

In all these sacraments it is a simple, visible sign that objectively guarantees the presence of the Holy

One, the blessing of the Redeemer. Thus through them the Church's *functionary* who performs this sign in the name of Christ and by the Church's commission, necessarily in some sense re-enters the domain of the supernatural, and acquires in some sense full powers whose ultimate basis can only be an express decision of our Lord's will and a special commission from Him. Thus the old character of the Catholic priesthood still clings to Luther's lay priesthood, in so far as an objectively efficacious sign of grace necessarily implies a minister objectively and effectively empowered to carry out this sign.

We cannot escape from the fact that wide tracts of Luther's thought were simply Catholic. The people who eliminated these Catholic elements from his message were the Lutheran theologians of the period of orthodoxy, especially in the late sixteenth and seventeenth centuries. There have always been on both sides theologians who, instead of protecting and promoting living religion, have endangered it. On both sides it has always been their habit to entangle living beliefs in bloodless abstractions, concepts and ideologies, and then to use the result as a ball to juggle with in polemic dispute. And when, having elaborated their systems of thought, they commit them to paper, it is usually with a bitter and choleric pen, and love is not in them. So it has always been. So it was then.

Luther himself, as we have seen, judged the doctrines, ordinances and usages of the Church according to their fitness for survival as he saw it: that is, according to whether they appeared to him to be loaded with gross abuses, or not. He suffered personally from the festering wounds in the Church and sought in his own fashion to heal them. It is true that he went about it, especially in the latter part of his life, with a self-assuredness and a cheerful readiness to assume responsibility which sometimes bordered on irresponsibility (Lortz, vol. i, p. 427). He was sometimes too ready simply to cut off the diseased limb instead of healing it. But his fundamental intention remained the healing and renewal of the ancient Church, not her dissolution and destruction. In the midst of his most violent attacks on Rome he said: "I may be mistaken; I am not a heretic" (Lortz, vol. i, p. 393). In the depths of his soul he was still, despite everything, bound to the Church, and that means to the Church as he then saw her, *ecclesia, una, sancta, catholica et apostolica.*

We find a very different attitude in the orthodox theology which gradually developed and established itself. It took the Lutheran doctrines out of their historical context, separated them from the ecclesiastical abuses with which they were bound up and presented them simply in themselves, as an abstract system of ideas, as the new Gospel in fundamental opposition to the old Gospel. Their expositions no longer envisaged the suffering Church, labouring under abuses, but simply the Church that had been. They were concerned to found and establish a completely new Church. Lutheran theology became radically anti-Catholic. It was therefore a special aim of their polemical writing to seize on all the Catholic elements which Luther had tolerated, and even expressly affirmed, and in the interests of the stylistic purity of their Lutheran doctrinal edifice ruthlessly to eliminate them. This de-Catholicizing process was pushed so far that to-day, as we have seen, Lutheran theologians who wish to bring their people back to Luther's own vision of the Church are accused of Catholicizing tendencies. Now indeed altar was set up against altar and Church against Church.

## The Papacy

But did not Luther himself, with unequalled savagery, attack the essential foundation of the Catholic Church, the "Rock" on which she is built? As early as the Leipzig Disputation in 1519 Luther had disputed the divine institution of the Papacy and its necessity for salvation, and from 1520 onwards he never tired of branding it as "the most poisonous abomination that the chief of devils has sent upon the earth".

That is indeed so. Papacy had no bitterer, no more determined foe than the barefoot friar of Wittenberg. He converted opposition and even hatred towards the Papacy into an essential element of Protestantism. The Rock which supports and safeguards the unity of the Church became in his teaching a rock on which that unity splits.

It is so to-day. There is no greater barrier to the union of German Christianity than the Roman Pope and his claim to have been called by God to be the Vicar of Christ and the Shepherd of all the faithful. All the theological difficulties that we have seen so far admit of at least a *possible* solution. But in this matter any such possibility seems excluded from the start. Why? Because in this matter not only men's minds but their very blood rise in revolt.

For centuries it was Germans who suffered most from the detestable strife which arose between the Papacy and the Emperors because of an unhappy confusion of religious and ecclesiastical issues with political and economic ones. The onset of externalism and worldliness which accompanied the Avignon captivity was and is felt by those of the Lutheran faith in a far deeper sense than by us Catholics. *We* make a sharp distinction between the person and the office. *They* see the crying scandal of a prolonged outrage against the majesty of the Holy

One, against the spirit of Christianity. Because their creed was born of the struggle against abuses identified with Catholicism, *protest* against the Catholic Church is an essential element of their whole religious attitude, the necessary foundation of their independent existence. But even in those Protestant circles where religion no longer speaks with the accents of Luther, opposition to the Papacy is firmly rooted. There is no sense in hiding this. That passion for independent thought, for the autonomy of the intellect, which was engrafted into the German soul by nineteenth-century idealist philosophy, sees in every papal command, every Roman decree, every book placed on the Index, a relapse into the Middle Ages and a threat to the basic rights of the human spirit.

As we have already stated, there is no possibility of *any* Christian rapprochement with the prophets or believers of "free thought". They are too small and narrow for us, and, however much they rave about the freedom of the intellect, they are not free enough for us. They are too small and narrow for us because they shut themselves up from the start in the limited world of phenomena, the world of appearances. They put artificial blinkers on eyes open to unconditioned, eternal reality, because they will not see the real world, the world of God, which brings forth the visible world and maintains it in being. Plato would say that one of their eyes is missing, the eye that perceives what is above and beyond the senses, the Reality of realities, the Mind of all mind.

We Christians cannot be content to share the vision of such moles. Even if the unfettered human intellect had attained to an understanding of all the forces and all the phenomena of this narrow little visible world and co-ordinated them in one system, we should feel in that system as in a cage. Again and again we should thrust our way through its bars to cry our *Sursum Corda*! For we Christians believe in a final, supreme meaning of all being and becoming. This Meaning is the living God. And we believe that the living God has opened Himself to us, in certain *homines religiosi,* the Patriarchs and Prophets, and at last in His Only-begotten Son; that He has opened to us the very depths of His being and of His inconceivable love. Standing within this love our souls can grow to their height and breadth. They grow free, incomparably freer than the purveyors of human freedom can ever become. For it is only in faith in the living God that we know that we are more excellent than the stream of cosmic forces and powers. We are above this stream, not below it. And it is only if we start from faith that we can read the riddle of existence and attain to a satisfactory understanding of the world and of our-

selves. It is only because we are children of God
that we are really free.

Union is only possible, then, where faith in the
living God and His Incarnate Son still binds and
strengthens consciences. It is only with *believing*
Protestants that we can discuss this final decisive
question: whether the Papacy was founded by the
will of Christ, or whether it is Antichrist who has
achieved an historical embodiment in it. For believing Christians this question can only be solved in the
light of Revelation, only, that is, by listening in
reverent fear to the Word of God, and to His Word
alone, not to personal preferences and feelings. No
anti-Roman sentiment should be allowed to decide
the question for us or accompany our consideration
of it. Ulrich von Hutten's diatribes against "foreign
priests" are understandable against the background
of the contemporary situation. All Germany was
completely "anti-Roman" then, as the Papal Nuncio
Aleander was himself compelled to report. The
policy of the Curia in matters of finance and official
appointments, and other things besides, had exas-
perated national instincts in the highest degree.

To-day there is no longer any just excuse for
regarding the religious question from the point of
view of national politics and giving it an answer
in those terms. The Renaissance tendency in Rome
came to an end, broadly speaking, with the frightful

visitation of the *sacco di Roma,* when the Eternal City was laid waste in May 1527. The Council of Trent and the great reforming Popes, Pius V, Gregory XII and Sixtus V, finally eradicated the abuses within the Church. Not one of Luther's accusations could justly be made to-day. Even the political dealings of the Roman See with secular princes have become impossible. No sober theologian would to-day accept Gregory VII's *Dictatus papae.* The Gregorian system, resting on presuppositions completely alien to our own, can be finally relegated to the past. It was the result of the medieval view of the world. On a deeper level, it resulted from the fact that the unity of Western Christendom was created by Rome alone, that its maintenance through the centuries was due solely to the authority of the Roman Pope, that the Emperor himself owed his numinous aspect entirely to his coronation by the Pope, and that it was common Christian belief that all matters of political, economic and cultural policy were from the moral point of view (*ratione peccati*) subject to the authority of the Roman See. The rise of the principle of nationality and the national states cut away a considerable area from the Gregorian system, and it was finally superseded by the new idea of the world and humanity introduced by the Renaissance. In consequence it is not possible nowadays for a Lutheran to keep his eyes on the abuses of the late Middle Ages and speak of the papal Antichrist as a mainstay for his own religious position.

Since the Council of Trent the idea of the Papacy has been tremendously spiritualized. It has become strictly religious, strictly Christian, strictly ecclesiastical, and the glorious image of the Vicar of Christ shines out from all the illustrious figures that have adorned the Papal throne since the great reforming Popes. As things are now, the question of the divine rights of the Papacy can be decided for the faithful *only in the light of Revelation.* Since the believing Protestant, with the overwhelming majority of modern theologians, cannot entertain doubts concerning the authenticity of Matt. xvi. 18–19, his conscience is clearly and seriously confronted by our Lord's words to Peter: ". . . I say to thee, that thou art the rock and upon this rock I will build my church, and the gates of hell shall not prevail against it, and I will give to thee the keys of the kingdom of heaven." He must face up to these words.

From the purely Biblical point of view it is indeed possible for him to think here of Peter *only,* not his successors or in particular his successors in Rome. But he will not wish nor be able to deny that there is another possible interpretation. For Christ's words are valid for all time. They are words of eternity. If the first generation had need of a rock if it was not to be defeated by the gates of hell, how much more would later centuries, threatened from all sides by schisms and heresies! Could Christ really have been considering only the few years in which Peter was to live? Would Christ not rather have been thinking of the Last Times which would be cut short by His coming and for which He wished to build an unconquerable Church? It is in any case *only in this sense* that Christianity afterwards understood Jesus' words concerning the rock and therefore called the See of Rome even from early Christian times the "See of Peter" (*cathedra Petri*). For it was convinced that Peter died as a martyr in Rome and was buried there, and that he lived on in his successors. It was in any case precisely the Church of Rome which from the time of Cyprian (d. 258), Irenaeus (d. 202) and even Ignatius of Antioch (d. circ. 110), was regarded as the chief Church of Christendom, as its true and unique centre of unity, creating and guaranteeing that unity.

As in the course of centuries the Church spread all over the world and the centrifugal forces, the forces of schism, grew stronger, so the inexhaustible vitality of the Church liberated centripetal forces too, and theologians understood more and more unambiguously and univocally the meaning of the Rock upon which Christ founded His Church. There is a great significance in the change which took place in the attitude of the greatest of the theologians of the end of the Middle Ages, the Cardinal Nicholas of Cusa. Like many of the theologians of the time, at the Councils of Constance and Basle he had, both in speech and in writing, supported Conciliarism, i.e., the superiority of a General Council to the Pope. But the lessons of Basle, the depressing realization that even the strongest religious desires do not prove themselves strong enough to create a unity of spirits, that there are situations so charged with explosive matter that even a General Council is no longer capable of reaching a united decision—all this drove him to the conclusion that amid the fluctuations of opinion there must be a last resort, a rock, to protect unity under *all* circumstances; a final, supreme religious authority, which *ex sese,* i.e., independently of the judgment of the bishops, can decide questions of faith and morals, and to which the whole Church is bound.

What Nicholas of Cusa discovered was to be learnt in the course of time by the whole of Christendom. We find ourselves confronted by the facts that alongside Luther appear Zwingli, Calvin and Thomas Münzer; that soon after Melanchthon's death the Lutheran Church was shaken by the crypto-Calvinists and Pietists; that in England, alongside the Anglican Church, Puritans, Presbyterians and Independents founded religious communions; and that to-day in America we can count more than three hundred sects tearing the Body of Christ to pieces. These facts practically force upon us the Catholic interpretation of Matt. xvi. 18, as finally developed at the Vatican Council in 1870.

It is the *inner necessity* of the Church, the constant threat and peril to her unity from human subjectivism, that necessitates this interpretation. For the sake of the unity of the Church the Rock of Peter's office must remain through the centuries, so that the Gates of Hell may not prevail. Seen from this viewpoint, the Roman Papacy and its claim to Apostolic authority cannot be an insuperable obstacle to the Christian confessions' coming together. For it is this Papacy alone which makes possible and realizes what all of us Christians must strive for, spiritual unity amongst ourselves.

## III

## THE CENTRAL QUESTION TO-DAY

WE CAN only speak in the full sense of unity in the Church if she stands upon *one* rock in submission to *one* shepherd. In the light of the development of the Western Church, this rock and this shepherd *can* only be the Bishop of Rome, whose See was hailed in the earliest Christian times as the *cathedra Petri*. Even distinguished Protestant historians like Salin and Kaspar do not attempt to deny that *belief* in the primacy, if not the *doctrine* of the primacy, goes back to the earliest Christian ages for which we have any evidence. The root of this belief is ultimately to be found in the early Christian view of the Church, in the conviction of the faithful that it was not they themselves, not their own Christian conscience nor their own interpretation of the Bible, but the authority of the Church alone that decided the question of salvation.

We have already pointed out that the first Christian communities were not founded by the written word but by the living teaching of the Apostles and their disciples, and that Christianity was already alive and flourishing before any Epistle or Gospel was written. From the beginning it was the *oral* teaching of the Apostles, not its crystallization in the Bible, which guaranteed the truth and clarity of the revelation.

From the literary point of view the Bible is a chance collection of missionary writings, inspired indeed by the Holy Ghost, but a chance collection nevertheless. It does not give a general view of revealed truths, a *Summa sacrae doctrinae* in the scholastic sense. Only in the Epistles to the Romans, the Ephesians and the Hebrews do we find a comprehensive development of ideas. But not even these Epistles give the whole of the Christian Gospel. Several of the apostolic letters have been lost, so that we have, for example, almost no information about the first eleven years of Paul's missionary activity.

The *whole* of revelation, the legacy of faith (*depositum fidei*), was entrusted from the beginning not to literary chance but to the personal responsibility of the Apostles and their successors. "O Timothy, keep that which is committed to thy trust," Paul exhorts his pupil (1 Tim. vi. 20). When the Gnostics appealed to mutilated or invented written texts, the decision against them did not come from Holy Writ but from the "rule of faith" (*regula fidei*), that is from the living, believing consciousness of the Church as preserved and transmitted by the bishops. Luther's *exclusive* esteem and reverence for Holy Writ is in contradiction with the facts of history. From the beginning we find, welling up between Christ and the Scriptures, the living teaching of the Church, guarding and explaining the truth. Through every gap and rift in the Biblical message gleam the clear waters of the stream of tradition, coursing through the Christian communities, guided and preserved by the bishops.

It is indeed *Christ* alone from whom all the Church's teaching proceeds and to whom it all points. Christianity is Christ. The teaching authority of the Church can do no more than draw on the riches of Christ. The Church has only to testify to the Lord's truth, not to create it. She is not herself the Light but is to give testimony of the Light. The Church's teaching activity is thus not creative. She generates no new truths of herself. She only takes the old truths, objectively given in Christ's revelation (explicitly or at the least in germ), and brings them into the subjective consciousness of the faithful.

We have arrived here at something essential which differentiates the Catholic from the Lutheran concept of the Church, and which provides the ultimate basis for the exclusiveness of the Catholic Church, her claim to be the one means of salvation. The believing Lutheran also recognizes that he is bound to his Church's confession of faith, to the ancient Christian creeds, to the Confession of Augsburg, perhaps to Luther's *Schmalkald Articles* and to the formula of 1580. But there is nothing absolute about this tie: the believing Lutheran does not simply and directly hear the word of Christ in the teaching of his Church.

It is truer to say that he does without the formularies of his Church in his *own* experience of Christ, when he encounters Him in his own conscience. And in so far as this experience of Christ in each separate believer necessarily remains dominated by subjective impressions, it is in the last analysis the *individual* conscience that determines the form and colour of each man's Christianity. His religious life does indeed gain something from this subjectivity— an interior dynamism, pressure and intensity; on the other hand, it lacks any ultimate assurance, any unconditional guarantee that it is really Christ and His Truth to whom the believer has given himself.

It is a quite different matter with the certainty of the believing Catholic. He is *unconditionally* bound to the teaching of the Church, because he is penetrated with the certainty that in the teaching of the Church he hears the word of Christ. He thus identifies the Church's message with the Gospel of our Lord. However humanly inadequate, however conditioned by the times the formularies of the

Church's teaching may be, they are yet for the Catholic conscience, in their deepest content, in their *substance*, brought out from the treasure of Christ.

In the strict sense this applies only to those truths which the Church expressly proclaims as truths of revelation. In the strict sense, then, it applies only to the realm of the Church's *dogmas*. But in so far as these dogmas do not exist in intellectual isolation but are connected both with each other and with truths in the natural order, the light of faith shines also upon their whole logical and historical context, and guarantees its certainty with varying degrees of intensity and logical strength according to the degree with which it is bound up with the dogmas themselves.

The other truths of faith which have been formulated in the course of centuries by the Church, though not clearly expressed in the Bible, are all contained at least in germ (*implicite*) in a revealed truth already clearly held and proclaimed by the teaching Church. They can all be shown to stand in an essential relationship to the Church's original, central dogma concerning Jesus the Christ. They have all, therefore, their assured place in the Christian message. They all had and have a salutary and creative effect upon the whole Christian body. They are all charged to-day with the devotion, the reverence and the atmosphere of living Christian faith. And we know that what lies behind all these dogmas is not the caprice of emotional piety nor mere historical chance but the clear teaching intention of the Church and behind her the message of Christ bearing testimony of Himself in her teaching.

We have come back to our starting point. We pointed out that the special character of the Catholic concept of the Church and the content of the Catholic faith lay in the identification of the Church's authority with the authority of Christ. The Church does not receive this authority indirectly, as though from the faith of the Christian communities honouring their Church as the teacher and witness of that faith. *Before* there were any communities with personal faith, and independently of them, when Christ founded His Church upon Peter, He constituted in Peter and with Peter the fullness of His own Messianic power. The Catholic sees in the office of teacher, priest and shepherd built upon Peter the continuation through the centuries of the Messianic authority of Christ Himself.

We must realize that, according to the testimony of the earliest sources, Christ did not attach this Messianic authority simply to the *personal* " pneuma " of His disciples, to their abundance of the Spirit. They were not His Apostles simply by virtue of being His disciples. For this they needed a special *com-*

87

*mission* from our Lord. "As the Father hath sent me, I also send you" (John xx. 21). This commission was given in the solemn act by which our Lord chose twelve from the multitude of His disciples to be His Apostles, exactly twelve, no more and no less, who were to transmit His Gospel to the twelve tribes of Israel. Thus our Lord organized the first Christian mission by the special call of the Twelve, the establishment of the college of Apostles. This college of Apostles is so much the one and only organ of the full powers of Christ that after Judas' suicide the election of Matthias had to take place to fill up the number of the Twelve. The fact that within this college, as we are shown in the Acts of the Apostles, Simon the son of John occupied a supereminent position, and that even in the Pauline communities he was referred to simply as "Rock", is not due to his personal qualities, to the strength of his faith, for instance, but again to a particular, explicit *call* by our Lord, which took place, as a consequence of the strength of his faith, in that solemn act at Caesarea Philippi (Matt. xvi. 18).

The very first Christian mission, the first preaching to the Jews, was not only a matter of the outpouring of the Spirit but of institutional means established by our Lord Himself—the college of the Twelve and the office of Rock. And, in the same way, later on it was not simply to all Christians filled with the

Spirit of the Lord, to all the men of the new faith
and love, that the office of preaching the Gospel fell.
On the contrary, unless an extraordinary charismatic
gift gave evidence of their prophetic vocation, they
must first receive *the laying on of hands* from the
Apostles. It was only by this laying on of hands
that they were numbered among the appointed witnesses of Christ (cf. Acts vi. 6; xiii. 3, etc.).

Thus from the beginning the spiritual basis of
Christianity, its striving for the fullness of the spirit
and interior perfection, was bound up with an
*institutional* element, the connection of the plenitude
of apostolic power with an impersonal super-personal
act, the laying on of hands. This turns our attention
away from the Self, from the personal qualities of
the believer, and directs them to the authority of
Christ, who alone sends labourers into the vineyard
and from whom alone comes all redemption. What
was later called the mission of the Church (*missio
canonica*) was from the very beginning an essential
element in the Christian message. "How shall they
preach unless they be sent?" (Rom. x. 15). Only
by the form of the laying on of hands did the believing Christian become a missionary, a witness of
the word, a steward of the mysteries. He bears the
full powers of Christ, but not so as to be in any sense
autonomous and dependent on himself. He is in no
sense the creative cause of our salvation, but only,

as theology expresses it, the "instrumental cause" (*causa instrumentalis*) and visible tool chosen by the Lord of the Church, with which He, our divine human Redeemer, invisibly communicates to the faithful the salvation which proceeds from the Trinity. The laying on of hands simply but effectively expressed the fact that the missionary had his place within the whole mission of Christ and partook of His powers. By this means he entered the "apostolic succession", entered into physical and historical contact with the first disciples and with Christ Himself, from whom every mission proceeds and who alone is its meaning and its object.

It is thus with reverent pride that the Catholic looks back on the long line of his bishops, for he knows that there is not one among them who could not historically show that he had been received into that apostolic lineage and so had entered into direct contact with Christ Himself. It is this apostolic succession of his bishops which guarantees to him that the stream of Christian tradition which brought forth and sustains the Bible is no wild torrent to break its banks and mingle with alien currents but that it was received at the beginning and conducted on its way by a strictly constituted channel, the unbroken unity of this same apostolic succession, leading straight back to Christ and guaranteeing the purity of the tradition received from Him.

Seen thus from within, the Church is primarily an *institution for salvation.* She is not simply a community of salvation, a community, that is, which receives in faith the salvation of Christ and carries it out in herself. It is she who *gives* this salvation and makes the faithful members of Christ. Thus she stands not only in a passive but also in an active relationship to Christ and the salvation He gives— always of course only as instrumental cause, as the visible earthly tool with which the Lord of the Church, who won her by His Blood, pours the treasures of grace and love proceeding from the Trinity into the body of the Church.

It is only because the Church is in this sense an institution for salvation that she can at the same time be a community of salvation. Her institutional, impersonal office constantly merges into the personal, the establishment of the Kingdom of God in the hearts of the faithful. The official side of the Church is never an end in itself, never self-idolatry, but always only a means and a *ministry,* a ministry to immortal souls. Simply because the Catholic sees in the Church's activity not the Church alone but ultimately Christ Himself at work, still teaching, still giving grace, still governing, his relationship to the official Church is a living religious thing, saturated with the same faith and the same love which he gives to Christ. What Eucken said of St. Augustine's concept of the Church is still true to-day of the life and experience of the Catholic: "All authority and every development of ecclesiastical power is sustained and embraced in intense personal living. The person in his direct relationship with God remains the animating spirit of the whole. Out from this life with God and into the order of the Church flows a constant stream of power, warmth and fervour which keeps it from sinking into a soulless automatism of ceremonial practice and activism. It is not the brute force of authority working by the sheer weight of its mere existence; there is an inner necessity insisting upon authority and sustaining it. It is chiefly out of these deep wells of life that the Church draws the immense power over consciences which she exercises down to this present day." (*Die Lebensanschauungen der grossen Denker*, 9th ed., p. 241.)

Catholicism means the closest possible fusion of the institutional and the personal, objective and subjective, office and spirit. And it is contrary to the essence of Catholicism when either of the two elements, whether the institutional or the personal, becomes exaggerated. In the balance of the two, in their organic relationship and interpenetration, lie the strength and life of the Catholic Church.

We must speak in more detail of this fundamental character of Catholicism if what follows is to be intelligible. The Catholic Church lives and breathes in the consciousness that by her apostolic succession founded upon Peter she stands in that stream of tradition which leads straight from Christ through the Apostles down to the present day. With this before her eyes she knows herself as divine tradition *incarnate,* as the visible embodiment of those powers of our Lord's Resurrection which are forever penetrating the world whether they were set down by the finger of God in Holy Writ or not. The Church has no need of witnesses. She witnesses to herself by the "divine tradition" in which she stands and by which she lives, indeed which she *is.*

Because of the way in which the message of Christ is thus united with her own tradition, the Catholic Church feels and knows herself as the Church of Christ in the emphatic, exclusive sense: as the visible revelation in space and time of the redemptive powers which proceed from Christ her Head, as the Body of Christ, as the *one means of salvation.* Because she is aware of this she is bound to condemn all other churches which have arisen or may arise —in so far as they are *churches,* i.e., sociological phenomena, and not merely a group of believers— as extra-Christian and indeed un-Christian and anti-Christian creations. To admit even the possibility that the final union of Christendom could take place other than in her and through her would be a denial and betrayal of her most precious knowledge that she is Christ's own Church. For her there is only one true union, reunion with herself.

For the Catholic the *immediate* object of all effort at reunion can only be that each according to his powers should help to remove the obstacles which are keeping those who do not believe in her from the Mother Church.

For these obstacles are his responsibility as well. It is not as though it were only the non-Catholic Christian who was the guilty party while the Catholic could think of himself as completely innocent and magnanimously proffering forgiveness. We made ourselves clear in our first section: both are at fault, and this fault extends to Rome itself.

Pope Adrian VI made public confession of this through his legate Chieregato before the German Princes assembled at the Reichstag at Nuremberg on the 3rd January 1523: "We freely acknowledge that God has allowed this chastisement to come upon His Church because of the sins of men and especially because of the sins of priests and prelates. . . . We know well that for many years much that must be regarded with horror has come to pass in this Holy See: abuses in spiritual matters, transgressions against the Commandments; indeed, that everything has been gravely perverted." And therefore he authorizes his legate to promise that "we will take all pains to reform, in the first place, the court of

Rome, from which perhaps all these evils take their origin ". When therefore the Holy See regards as one of its gravest and most urgent tasks the restoration of unity to Christendom—not only with the Orthodox Churches, which already have the essentials of dogma, cult and organization in common with it, but also with the Protestant communions—it is thereby fulfilling not only the duty of the Good Shepherd setting out in pursuit of the lost sheep but also the special duty of common penance and expiation.